WIND AND AIR

REVISED AND UPDATED

PRESSURE

Measuring the Weather

Alan Rodgers and Angella Streluk

www.heinemann.co.uk/library

Visit our website to find out more information about Heinemann Library books.

To order:

☎ Phone 44 (0) 1865 888066

🖹 Send a fax to 44 (0)1865 314091

💻 Visit the Heinemann Library Bookshop at www.heinemann.co.uk/library to browse our catalogue and order online.

First published in Great Britain by Heinemann Library, Halley Court, Jordan Hill, Oxford OX2 8EJ, part of Harcourt Education.
Heinemann Library is a registered trademark of Harcourt Education Ltd.

Editorial: Joanna Talbot
Design: Michelle Lisseter and Philippa Jenkins
Picture Research: Ruth Blair
Production: Julie Carter

Originated by Chroma Graphics
Printed and bound in China by South China Printing Company Limited

ISBN 978 0 431 03853 7
12 11 10 09 08
10 9 8 7 6 5 4 3 2 1

British Library Cataloguing in Publication Data
Rodgers, Alan
Wind and air pressure. - (Measuring the weather)
1. Winds - Measurement - Juvenile literature
2. Air pressure - Measurement - Juvenile literature
I. Title II. Streluk, Angella
551.5'18
A full catalogue record for this book is available from the British Library.

Acknowledgements
The publishers would like to thank the following for permission to reproduce photographs: Alan Rodgers p. **27**; Amington Heath Community School/Alan Rodgers p. **19**; Bruce Coleman Collection p. **14**; Corbis/George Hall p. **25**; D Offiler p. **18**; FLPA p. **9**; Photocopy p. **7**; Robert Harding p. **8**; Science Photo Library p. **24**; Stone pp. **4**, **10**, **21**; The Met Office p. **16**; Trevor Clifford Photography pp. **6**, **15**, **26**.

Cover photographs reproduced with permission of Photodisc and Tudor Photography.

Our thanks to Jacquie Syvret of the Met Office for her assistance during the preparation of this book, and to Amington Heath Community School.

Every effort has been made to contact copyright holders of any material reproduced in this book. Any omissions will be rectified in subsequent printings if notice is given to the publishers.

Disclaimer
All the Internet addresses (URLs) given in this book were valid at the time of going to press. However, due to the dynamic nature of the Internet, some addresses may have changed, or sites may have changed or ceased to exist since publication. While the author and publishers regret any inconvenience this may cause readers, no responsibility for any such changes can be accepted by either the author or publishers.

Contents

You can find words in bold, **like this**, in the Glossary.

What is wind?

Wind is one of the most important features of our weather. Wind can bring rain, and it can cause hot or cold weather. It is one of the main features of storms. In this book, you will find out how the wind works and what effect it has on the weather.

When we feel the wind on our faces, we are feeling the movement of air. Wind is an **air mass** that moves from one area to another. Air from **high air pressure** areas always flows to **low air pressure** areas. The greater the difference in pressure between the areas, the stronger the wind will be.

Why is the pressure of air different in different areas? Changes in **air pressure** are linked to the amount of sun an area gets. If an area gets lots of sun, the air becomes hot, rises and leaves a space that needs filling. Air comes in to fill this space, causing a wind. The Sun is therefore the driving power behind air pressure and the wind.

Wind plays a part in some enjoyable activities. Children enjoy flying kites. Adults also enjoy sports that depend on the wind. These include hang-gliding and sailing, where the direction of the wind is very important.

Weather and climate

Many people need to know what the weather will be. Sometimes, wind can be very dangerous. It can cause damage and injury to property and people. So scientists, called **meteorologists**, measure the weather and try to predict what it will do in the future. Meteorologists around the world try to record the information in the same way so everyone can share and understand it. They show some of their weather information in weather reports, using sets of symbols like those shown in the diagram below. The symbols used are usually ones that can easily be understood by anybody. Sometimes they are not quite the same, even in the same country, but if you know what one set means, it is usually easy to see what another set means, too.

In any one place, the weather changes a lot over a long period of time. By recording these patterns in the change of weather, weather watchers can describe a place's **climate**. Climate is the weather in a place over a large number of years.

Be careful!

Do not look directly at the Sun when studying the weather. Never shelter under trees during a thunderstorm, as they may be hit by lightning.

These are the symbols used by meteorologists throughout the world to represent wind speeds. They are added to **station circles** *like the one in the diagram to show the wind direction in a particular place.*

Weather symbols: wind speed and direction

Symbol	Speed	Symbol	Speed
Calm	Calm		23–27 knots
	1–2 knots		28–32 knots
	3–7 knots		33–37 knots
	8–12 knots		38–42 knots
	13–17 knots		43–47 knots
	18–22 knots		48–52 knots

station circle showing wind speed and direction

Wind direction

Knowing the direction that the wind comes from is an important part of measuring the weather. We can watch flags and trees to see which way the wind is blowing. However, scientists need to measure the wind in a more accurate way. One of the simplest and oldest weather recording devices is the **weather vane**, like the one shown below.

The pointed end of the weather vane is the most important part. It tells us which way the wind is coming from – not where it is going to. The wind blows the larger sail end until the vane is in line with the wind, and does not block the wind anymore. Sometimes, the wind can change direction and catch the sail from a different way. If the wind changes in a clockwise direction, it **veers**. If it changes in an anti-clockwise direction, it **backs**. If the wind keeps changing direction like this, watch the vane for 30 seconds. Then decide which way the vane has pointed for most of the time you have been watching it.

TRY THIS YOURSELF!

Ask an adult to help you make a simple weather vane.

pointer

sail

washer

- Make a card sail fixed to a stick pointer.
- Mount the pointer on an upright piece of wood. Use a washer so that it can turn freely. Be sure to balance the pointer, as the sail end will be heavier than the pointer end.
- Make labels for north, south, east, and west.
- Weight a plastic bottle with water or stones to make a base.
- Place the vane carefully so that nothing obstructs a free flow of wind around it. Set it up in an open space away from obstacles such as hedges, fences, and buildings.
- Use a compass to turn the direction labels so that they point correctly.

Electronic devices

Wind direction can also be measured by electronic devices. Some are labelled with the directions of the compass and show the direction with a pointer. Other devices use a digital display that shows the wind direction as degrees of a circle. For example, north is 360°, east is 90°, south is 180°, and west is 270°.

*Use your data from your weather vane to fill in a "wind rose". Colour in a square each day along the line for the wind direction of that day. At the end of several weeks of observation you will see if there is a **prevailing** wind. Here, the prevailing wind is from the northeast. Remember, when there is no wind, no direction can be recorded.*

Land and sea

People often go to the seaside on hot sunny days to enjoy the cool sea breezes. These breezes are caused by the difference in the temperature of the land and the sea. The ground and air heat up at different speeds. The ground and sea also heat up at different speeds. This brings about winds called land and sea breezes.

Sea breezes

Sea breezes are light winds that travel from the sea to the land. During the day the land warms up quickly in the Sun. The sea warms up more slowly. In the summer, the difference between the temperature of the land and sea can be quite big. This causes the air to move in a large **cycle**.

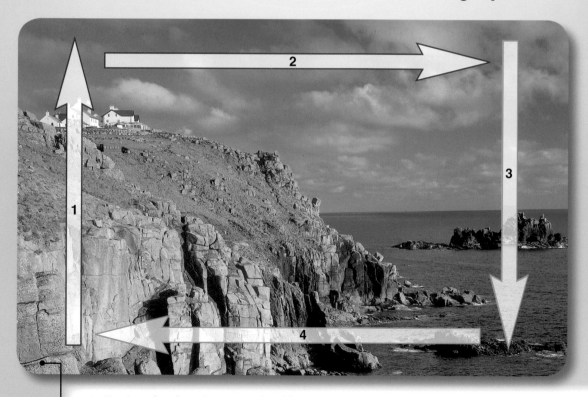

1. During the day, the warm land heats the air above it, which then rises. This causes an area of **low air pressure**, which is ready to be filled by more air.
2. The warm air, high in the sky, goes out to sea.
3. At sea, the warm air is cooled and sinks back down.
4. The cooler air from the sea comes in to take the place of the warm air. This is the sea breeze we feel. The cycle continues.

The biggest difference in temperature is during the afternoon, and this is when the sea breezes will be strongest.

Land breezes

Land breezes are the opposite of sea breezes. At night, the land cools down quite quickly compared to the sea. The air above the sea is warmer than that over the land, and it rises, creating an area of low air pressure. This causes a breeze from the land to the sea.

The difference between land and sea temperatures at night is not as great as during the day. This means that land breezes are not as strong as sea breezes, but ships near the coast may notice them. These breezes also occur at the edge of large lakes. These are known as lake breezes.

1. *At night, the sea cools down quite slowly compared to the land. The air above the sea is warmed. It rises, creating an area of low air pressure.*
2. *Cool air from the land moves in to fill the space left by rising air over the sea.*
3. *The warm air from high above the sea moves towards the land.*
4. *The warm air sinks as it cools over the land. It takes the place of the air that went out to sea.*

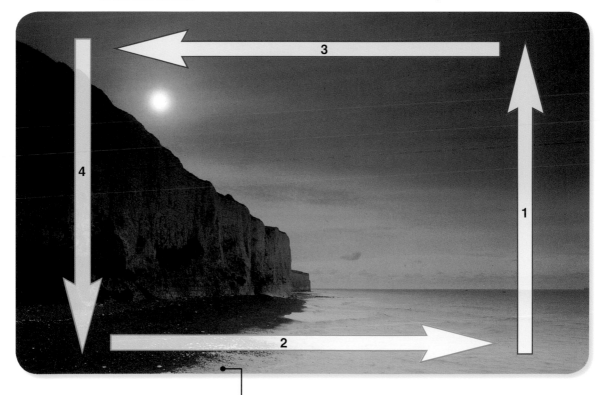

This cycle continues as long as there is a difference in temperature between the sea and land.

Wind chill

Sometimes, a day might feel really cold, even though the temperature is not very low. We especially notice that our face gets cold when the wind blows on it. Heat given off by the skin warms the air close to our face, but when the wind blows hard, it drives away the warmth. The way the wind cools things down like this is known as wind chill.

*Two places close to each other, but at very different heights, will have very different temperatures. The people standing at the foot of the mountain do not need coats. At the top of the mountain, at the same time, this walker needs to wear more clothing. The extra clothes protect him against the combined effects of wind chill and being at a higher **altitude**.*

High and low

On a summer day it might feel quite warm at the bottom of a mountain. People may be wearing light clothing. But if they travel up the mountain, they will find it feels much colder largely because of wind chill. The very strong winds found on tops of hills and mountains blow away heat from people. It feels very cold indeed. People have died from the cold, because they thought a warm day at the bottom of a mountain meant that it would feel the same at the top.

Working out wind chill

In cold climates, serious walkers and people working outside use a Wind Chill Equivalent Temperature Chart to find out how cold it is going to feel. This difference between the real temperature and what the temperature feels like is known as the wind chill factor. For example, an air temperature of 8 °C (46.4 °F)with a wind speed of 20 kph (12 mph) will mean that the wind chill equivalent temperature will be 0 °C (32 °F). As a general rule, the stronger the wind, the cooler it will feel.

		Air Temperature							
		8°C	4°C	0°C	−4°C	−8°C	−12°C	−16°C	−20°C
	Calm	8	4	0	−4	−8	−12	−16	−20
Wind Speed (kph)	10	5	0	−4	−8	−13	−17	−22	−26
	20	0	5	−10	−15	−21	−26	−31	−36
	30	−3	−8	−14	−20	−25	−31	−37	−43
	40	−5	−11	−17	−23	−29	−35	−41	−47
	50	−6	−12	−18	−25	−31	-37	−43	−49
	60	−7	−13	−19	−26	−32	−39	−45	−51

Wind chill can be worked out using this table. To read it you need to know the temperature (taken out of the wind) and the strength of the wind. Trace down from the correct temperature and across from the wind speed. The figure given where they meet is the temperature that will be felt.

Wind and weather

When forecasting the weather, you will need to know where you are in relation to the land and sea around you. Whether you are near the sea or in the centre of a large area of land will affect the weather you get. Generally, if a wind is **maritime** and has blown over the sea, it will "collect" a lot of moisture from the sea. Air that is warm will hold more moisture than cooler air. If a wind has come from a warm place, then it will bring warm weather. If a wind has blown over **continental** land, then the wind will generally be drier. Wind that has blown from a cold part of the world, such as the polar regions, will be colder.

The four main types of air masses		
	Warm	**Cold**
Land	Continental tropical (cT)	Continental polar (cP)
Sea	Maritime tropical (mT)	Maritime polar (mP)

The chart above shows the technical terms for air masses. These terms depend on where the wind comes from. Which winds are likely to bring rain? When might dry weather be brought by wind? The map gives an example showing the expected types of wind for four wind directions affecting London, UK. Can you tell which winds should have which terms from the chart?

cold and wet

cold and dry

warm and wet

warm and dry

Mountain and valley breezes

In many places the shape of the land causes different winds. Mountain and valley breezes are examples of this. During the day, sunlight warms the sides of a valley. This causes air to rise up the slopes. This makes a gentle rising breeze, known as a valley breeze. At night, the mountain slopes cool quickly, and they cool the air near them. This cool air is dense, so it sinks down into the valley. This movement of air is called a mountain breeze.

Sometimes, air is warmed when it flows down the sides of mountains. One example is the Chinook, a wind which comes down the eastern slopes of the Rocky Mountains in North America. Because this wind is dry and warm, it can melt snow from railway tracks and uncover prairies for grazing. In New Zealand, the Canterbury Northwester is a similar type of wind. It blows down the mountains, taking warm air to the Pacific Ocean.

Daytime

rising air

Night-time

sinking air

As the air warms up during the day, it rises from the valleys and up onto the mountains. This creates a valley breeze. As the air cools at night, it sinks down the hills and into the valleys. This creates a mountain breeze.

Measuring wind strength

Knowing the correct wind speed can be very important. For example, people parachuting for the first time are only allowed to jump if there is no more than a gentle wind. Aeroplane pilots also need to know how strong winds are when they are taking off and landing, so that they can adjust their controls.

Wind measuring devices are called **anemometers**. There are many different types of anemometer. Some will also tell you the direction of the wind, because they have small compasses built into them. Other anemometers may have a tube with a small indicator inside it that is lifted by the wind. There is a scale next to the tube, which shows the wind speed.

How to measure wind speed

To measure the wind, stand in an open space, making sure that there are no buildings or trees nearby. Stand with the strongest wind on your left and hold out your wind measuring device with your arm out straight.

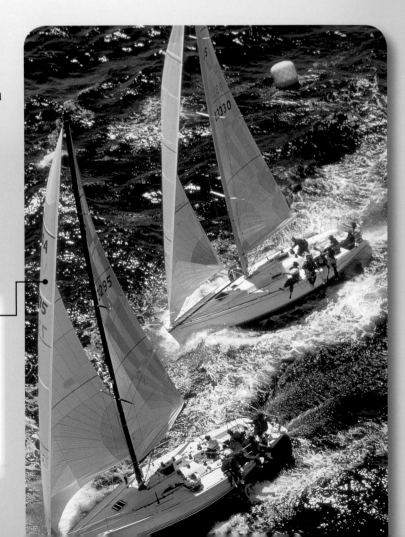

*Many modern boats have an automatic **weather station** that includes an anemometer. This is especially important if the boats are going on long journeys.*

This will help to stop your body disturbing the wind. Watch the indicator for one minute and make a note of the readings every fifteen seconds. Find the average by adding up your four readings and then dividing the sum by four. When the wind blows harder for a short time it is called a gust. Gusts should also be recorded. They will give readings that are higher than most of the other readings taken at the same time.

It is important that an anemometer is used away from any obstructions, such as trees or buildings. Obstructions may speed up or slow down the wind before it gets to the anemometer, giving incorrect readings.

DID YOU KNOW?

Wind speed can by recorded as:
- metres or feet per second
- kilometres or miles per hour
- **knots** (nautical miles per hour)

Once the speed is known, the correct Beaufort scale reading (see pages 16–17) can be worked out.

A hand-held anemometer can be very accurate. The wind meter shown in this picture is a small and light anemometer. Modern electronic portable weather monitors like the one on the far right can record wind gusts and average wind speed. They can also calculate wind chill.

The Beaufort wind scale

Up until about 150 years ago, most ships relied on the wind to make them move. Sailors needed to know what the wind was like so they would know which sails to put up. If it had too many sails up, the ship would blow over. If it had too few sails up, the ship would not be able to reach its best speed. Unfortunately, there were no standard descriptions of wind strengths. Then, in 1805, Sir Francis Beaufort made a scale to describe what the sea looked like when the wind was at different strengths. He did this mainly by describing how high the waves were. A similar scale was later made for use on land. This is what many weather watchers use today.

Reading the Beaufort scale

The **Beaufort scale** tries to make it easy to describe wind strength accurately. Each strength has a number, a description, and the wind speed. There are also a few words to describe what the user can see, which help in choosing the correct number on the scale. The wind speed is given in kilometres per hour (kph) and miles per hour (mph) for weather forecasts, but for ships and aircraft it is given in **knots**. One knot is equal to 1.85 kph or 1.15 mph.

Sir Francis Beaufort (1774–1857) was born in Ireland. He was the first person to use descriptions of the sea to work out the strength of the wind.

BEAUFORT SCALE

Number and description	Features	Air speed kph (mph)
0 calm	smoke rises vertically, water smooth	less than 1 (less than 1)
1 light air	smoke shows wind, direction water ruffled	1–5 (1–3)
2 light breeze	leaves rustle, wind felt on face	6–11 (4–7)
3 gentle breeze	loose paper blows around	12–19 (8–12)
4 moderate breeze	branches sway	20–29 (13–18)
5 fresh breeze	small trees sway, leaves blown off	30–39 (19–24)
6 strong breeze	whistling in telephone wires	40–50 (25–31)
7 near gale	large trees sway	51–61 (32–38)
8 gale	twigs break from trees	62–74 (39–46)
9 strong gale	branches break from trees	75–87 (47–54)
10 storm	trees uprooted, weak buildings collapse	88–102 (55–63)
11 violent storm	widespread damage	103–116 (64–72)
12 hurricane	widespread structural damage	above 116 (above 72)

The Beaufort scale means that you don't need an **anemometer** to estimate the wind strength. You can observe your surroundings. If the leaves on the trees are rustling, then you may note that it is a 2 on the scale, a light breeze of about 8 kph (5 mph) on average. If you can see large branches moving on the trees then it may be a number 6 on the scale. This means the wind is blowing at 40–50 kph (25–31 mph).

Using technology to monitor the wind

It is possible to use quite simple items of electronic equipment to measure the wind. **Raw data** is most useful when it is analysed to make charts and graphs. The simple data you collect can then help you show how weather changes over time, or weather **trends**.

You will often see **anemometers** at airports, by railways, on high bridges, near ports, and on tall buildings. Many are linked to electronic monitoring systems and computers. These systems can collect the data, save it and display the wind speed. Some anemometers are placed out at sea and they may send their data, by satellite, to **monitoring stations**.

Using an anemometer

You can use an anemometer and a computer to find the best place to put wind monitoring equipment. Different wind speeds can be recorded in different locations, even within small areas. The effects of buildings, trees, and other obstacles can affect the force of the wind.

Although it is easier to place anemometers on land, the more useful ones may be those out at sea on ships. These are of great importance in monitoring incoming weather.

These obstructions do not always slow the wind down. When there are small gaps between buildings, wind speed can actually increase, because the gaps squeeze the wind through faster. People who live in cities with tall buildings know about this. Weather watchers normally position their anemometers 10 metres (33 feet) above the ground to avoid the effects of buildings and other obstacles.

Anemometers are easy to use, even for young children. These students are investigating the difference in wind strength in different locations. They could change the height of the anenometer in one location to see if the wind speed is different.

TRY THIS YOURSELF!

Investigate wind speed by measuring the wind strength in different locations.

- Select a few places where you think the wind speed will be different. Mark these on a map.
- Measure the wind speed for a set period of time in the various different locations.
- Enter the data into a spreadsheet program to graph it.
- Look at the graphs to see what similarities and differences you can spot.

Extreme winds

Some winds can be very dangerous and cause lots of damage. Terrible storms happen all over the world. They are called different names in different places. Hurricanes are storms starting in the warm southern part of the North Atlantic or eastern North Pacific Oceans. Similar storms in the China Seas and western North Pacific area are called typhoons. In India and Australia, these storms are called **cyclones**. All these storms are known internationally as tropical cyclones. Tropical cyclones happen in the warmer seasons, when the conditions are right. Wind and rain, combined with a drop in **atmospheric pressure**, creates a revolving storm which can cause terrible damage. Tropical cyclones are 500–800 kilometres (300–500 miles) across, with a minimum wind speed of 64 **knots**. In 2005, one very strong hurricane, Hurricane Katrina, and the subsequent floods caused the deaths of at least 1,800 people in the Mississippi delta in the United States.

The most destructive storms occur mainly in tropical regions. They usually start over the oceans. Data from satellites is used to give warnings, wherever possible, of forthcoming storms. The blue arrows on this map show where the various types of storms generally occur.

Tornadoes

Tornadoes are caused by moist warm air rising rapidly at about 160 kph (100 mph) and can start as thunderstorms. The movement of air between different areas of pressure causes winds at the top of the storm to spin. They develop into a twisting column of wind that picks up dust and debris from the ground. The dust and debris travels up and down the column, and makes it look dark.

There is a big difference in **air pressure** inside the column compared to outside it. This difference means that if it passes directly over a building, the building can be damaged. Along with the very strong winds this air pressure difference makes a tornado very destructive. Tornadoes are so strong that they are measured on a special scale called the Fujita Scale for Damaging Wind. Hurricanes are measured on the Saffir-Simpson Hurricane Damage Potential Scale.

"Waterspouts" and "dust devils" are the smaller sea and land versions of these storms. Waterspouts do not rotate as quickly as tornadoes and happen only over the sea. Dust devils form on clear hot days when warm air rises from a hot surface. They are mostly small and last only a brief time. In Australia, these are known as "Willy-willys", which is an Aboriginal term.

This whirling spiral of wind is very dark, because it is full of debris that it has sucked up. Nobody would want to photograph a tornado from very close, as it is extremely dangerous.

Global winds

So far we have looked at winds that happen close to land. But high in the **atmosphere** there are other winds. The main cause of these high **altitude** winds is the differences in temperature in different parts of the world. For example, hot air rises at the equator. Cooler air takes its place, and this creates wind.

This difference in temperatures creates a regular system of air movements called the "Hadley cells". For example, in the tropics winds always flow westwards, creating what is known as the trade winds. For hundreds of years sailors have known about these winds, and used them to plan their voyages. Some areas, especially on the equator, never have these winds and are known as the doldrums.

Jet streams

These 'rivers of wind' flow in particular directions and areas of the globe and their speeds vary. They were dicovered during World War II when aeroplanes began to fly at higher altitudes. The jet streams flow in a generally easterly direction, although they travel in wavy patterns.

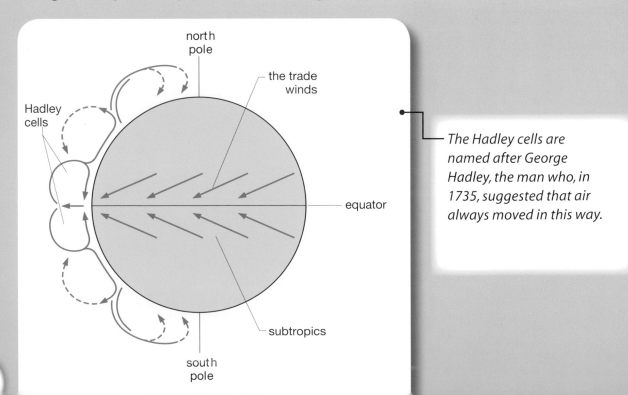

north pole

the trade winds

Hadley cells

equator

The Hadley cells are named after George Hadley, the man who, in 1735, suggested that air always moved in this way.

subtropics

south pole

Meteorologists use **weather balloons** to measure these winds. This helps to predict their effects on the weather. It also provides information for aeroplanes that fly high up in the sky.

El Niño

One of the trade winds makes water move in the South Pacific Ocean. A current of surface water is carried west. This allows cold water to come up from further down in the ocean. This brings up nutrients that feed sea life off the west coast of South America. Every few years the trade winds weaken, changing the temperature and rainfall patterns over a large area. It also means that the direction of the South Pacific equatorial current changes. This prevents the rising of the cold water and nutrients, and it also brings a current of warm water to the coast of Peru. When this happens, the **climate** in a large area is affected. This effect is known generally as El Niño.

During an El Niño

drought occurs in western Pacific

trade winds reversed

heavy rains affect eastern Pacific

South America

Australia

South Pacific equatorial current reversed

cold deep waters are prevented from reaching the surface by warm waters carried from the western Pacific

A reversal in the South Pacific equatorial current is called an El Niño. Because weather events are usually connected, the current reversal has an effect on a wider area. This diagram shows what happens during an El Niño.

What is air pressure?

Air pressure is the weight of air pressing down. Did you know that 1 square metre of air weighs 10,000 kilograms (22,046 pounds) on the ground? Imagine this much weight on your head! You don't feel this weight because you have air inside you that is at the same pressure as the air outside.

You can feel this air inside you if you travel in an aeroplane. The air pressure changes quickly, and the air pressure on each side of your eardrum does not have time to readjust. Eventually, your ear will "pop" as the pressure suddenly becomes the same.

Blaise Pascal (1623–1662) thought that air had weight. So he sent his friend up a mountain to measure the air pressure at the top, and compared it to the air pressure at the bottom. There was a big difference and this helped to prove his theory.

The diagram below shows the difference in air pressure at the top and bottom of a mountain that is 1,000 metres (3,280 feet) high. There is much less pressure at the top.

915 millibars
(91.5 kiloPascals)

1,040 millibars
(104 kiloPascals)

mountain

Height in metres

1,000
800
600
400
200
0

TRY THIS YOURSELF!

- Hang a coat hanger up and make sure it balances evenly.
- Take two identical balloons.
- Blow up one of the balloons.
- Hang a balloon on each end of the coat hanger.
- The end with the blown-up balloon goes down. This shows that air has mass (weight).

Different pressures

The air in different parts of the world is at different pressures. Weather forecasters show the difference in air pressure on their maps by drawing lines that join areas of the same air pressure together. These lines are called isobars. In simple terms, low-pressure areas are caused by rising warm air. High-pressure areas are caused by falling cold air. Air from high-pressure areas moves to take the place of the rising air in low-pressure areas. We feel this air movement as wind.

Aeroplanes use air pressure to tell how high they are. Pilots need to regularly contact local air traffic controllers to find out the current air pressure of an area. They then need to adjust their instruments to the correct reading. They can then navigate accurately, avoiding obstacles such as mountains.

Barometers

You can measure **air pressure** using a barometer. **Mercury** barometers measure the effect of air pressure on a tube of mercury. This is read using a scale. Another type, which is more convenient and popular, is called an **aneroid** barometer. This works by measuring the pressure of the air on a sealed unit which has had much of its air sucked out.

Aneroid barometers can be placed indoors so they can be conveniently read. Although they are indoors they measure the pressure of the **atmosphere** outside. However, they should not be placed near any strong draughts. The draughts will change the pressure and cause the barometer to give incorrect readings.

Many barometers have descriptions of the weather written by the scales. These are not as useful as they seem. They only provide a very rough guide to forthcoming weather, or tell you about the weather as it is. When it is stormy, you will not need a barometer to tell you!

*A barometer looks like a clock, but it measures air pressure, not time. Scientific barometers have their scale in **millibars** (mb for short) or **kiloPascals** (kPa), but some have it in inches.*

Using a barometer

Read the barometer by looking at the pointer and making a note of its position. Gently tap the face of the barometer and see how much it moves, and whether it is rising or falling. The average reading should be about 1013 millibars or 101.3 kiloPascals. A very low reading might be 960 millibars or 96 kiloPascals. A very high reading might be 1040 millibars or 104 kiloPascals. When you have made a few readings, every three hours or so, you can make some predictions about the approaching weather, using the table below.

Chart of barometer readings and the weather they bring	
Pointer movement	**Weather prediction**
Rapid fall in air pressure	Stormy weather
Steady – little change in air pressure	Weather the same as before
Steady rise in air pressure	Fine weather

This type of barometer is called a barograph. A pen on the end of an arm records the air pressure on a revolving chart. This chart will record a week's data. The line shows the rising and falling air pressure.

Highs and lows

You can find out what will happen to the weather from weather forecasts on the radio, television, in newspapers and magazines, and on the Internet. Much of the information is shown on maps called charts. The charts that show **air pressure** are called isobar charts.

You will often see the lines called isobars on a weather map. These lines join together places with the same air pressure, measured in **millibars** or **kiloPascals**. If the lines are close to each other, then the pressure will change a lot over a short distance. This means there are strong winds there.

If the measurement for the air pressure on the weather map is under 1000 millibars (100 kiloPascals), this indicates low pressure. The middle of an area of **low air pressure** is called a **cyclone**. There will be a lot of rain and showers there. In winter, this could also mean snow or hail is on its way.

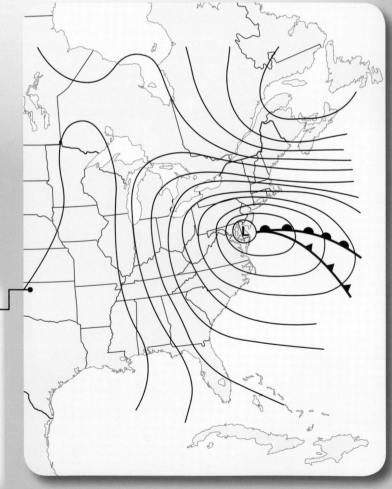

*The line between two **air masses** is called a **front**. Triangles are used to label a cold front. Semi-circles on the lines indicate a warm front. You can see these features on this map and on weather maps on television and in newspapers.*

When the measurement for the air pressure on the weather map is between 1025 and 1050 millibars (102.5–105 kiloPascals), this indicates high pressure. The middle of an area of high pressure is called an **anti-cyclone**. In the summer, when the weather map shows few isobar lines, it will be windless and settled. In the winter, the same isobars may mean fog and/or frost.

Fronts

Lines with triangles or semicircles on them show where air of different temperatures meets. If there are blue triangles, it means that cold air is pushing warm air. This is called a cold front. A cold front forces the warm air up and brings stormy, often thundery weather. If you see red semi-circles, it means that warm air is pushing cold air. This is called a warm front. The warm air slowly rises over the cold air and brings rain.

Cold and warm air eventually mix together to make what is called an occluded front. This is where the stronger of the two fronts has overtaken the weaker front. The weather underneath will be very unpleasant and stormy.

Wind and air pressure are linked together, with one influencing the other. As the wind can carry different weather, hot or cold, wet or dry, it is an important factor in the meteorologists' work.

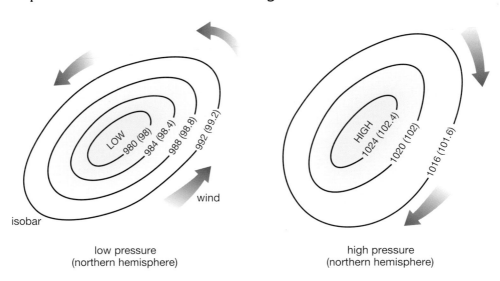

low pressure
(northern hemisphere)

high pressure
(northern hemisphere)

In the northern hemisphere, the wind blows clockwise round a high-pressure area and anti-clockwise around a low-pressure area. In the southern hemisphere, the directions are reversed. These diagrams show the wind directions in the northern hemisphere. The measurements on each diagram show the air pressure in millibars (kiloPascals in brackets).

Glossary

air mass body of air, in which all the air is of approximately the same temperature and humidity

air pressure pressure at the surface of the Earth caused by the weight of the air in the atmosphere

altitude height, usually measured from sea level

anemometers instruments for measuring wind strength

aneroid describes a barometer which does not use liquid to monitor air pressure. Instead it uses a sealed unit which has had most of the air sucked out. This is called a partial vacuum.

anti-cyclone system of winds blowing in a spiral around a centre of high pressure

atmosphere gases that surround our planet

atmospheric pressure another term for air pressure

backs changes of wind direction in an anti-clockwise direction

Beaufort scale system of recording wind speed, devised by Francis Beaufort in 1805. It is a numerical scale ranging from 0 to 12, calm being indicated by 0 and a hurricane by 12.

climate weather conditions in a place over a long period of years

continental describes a wind that comes from a large land mass

cycle set of events which happen one after the other in the same order, over and over again

cyclone system of winds blowing in a spiral around a centre of low pressure

front front edge of an air mass, where it meets air of a different temperature

high air pressure reading on the barometer of between 1025 and 1050 millibars, or 102.5 and 105 kiloPascals

kiloPascal measurement of air pressure. One kiloPascal is equal to 10 millibars.

knots nautical miles per hour, used in navigation and meteorology

low air pressure reading on the barometer of between 950 and 975 millibars, or 95 and 97.5 kiloPascals

maritime to do with the sea

mercury silvery metal that is a liquid at ordinary temperatures

meteorologist a person who studies the weather by gathering and analysing data

millibar measurement of air pressure often used on barometers

monitoring stations places where weather data is received and used for weather forecasts

prevailing the most common or frequent one

raw data information that has not been analysed

station circle collection of symbols used by meteorologists to show local weather conditions

trends repeated patterns in the observed weather

veers changes of wind direction in a clockwise direction

weather balloons large balloons filled with a gas that makes them rise through the air. They carry various weather instruments that send data back to meteorologists.

weather station collection of weather instruments that measure the weather regularly

weather vane instrument that is used to show which direction the wind is coming from

Find out more

Which wind direction brings the most rain to your area? When you complete the wind rose activity on page 7 note down when it rains alongside the wind direction. Is there a pattern? Look on a map to see what is at the eight points of the compass from your location. Does it explain your results?

Read how to take air pressure readings and how you should note whether the air pressure is rising, falling or constant. Make a note of the type of weather which goes with each day's recordings. What do you notice when the air pressure goes up steadily? What do you notice if there is a rapid fall? Be patient and you will observe some interesting results.

Watch out in the news and on the Internet for storms. Plot them on a map showing their strength, name, and dates. Collect cuttings and interesting facts. Look at satellite images of the storms. Where do most of the storms occur? Is there a time of the year when storms are more frequent? Is it the same in all continents and both hemispheres?

Websites

http://www.weatherwizkids.com/
Weather Wiz Kids has good information on storms, wind and much more. Compare the Beaufort scale description on this site with the one on page 17.

http://www.amingtonheath.staffs.sch.uk/intro.html
The Staffordshire School Weather Data Site has good ideas for collecting data and for setting up your own weather station. You can also follow a link to help you build a simple weather station.

More books to read

Wild Weather: Tornado, Catherine Chambers (Heinemann Library, 2007)
Discovering Geography: Weather, Rebecca Hunter (Raintree, 2003)
Science on File: Weather, Richard and Louise Spilsbury (Evans, 2006)

Index